I CAN BE A
CHEF

By Ann Heinrichs Tomchek

Prepared under the direction of Robert Hillerich, Ph.D.

CHILDRENS PRESS ®

CHICAGO

Library of Congress Cataloging in Publication Data
Tomchek, Ann Heinrichs.
   I can be a CHEF.
   Includes index.
   Summary: Explores the world of those who cook for a
living, examining where they work and what they do in
preparing meals for others.
   1. Cookery—Vocational guidance—Juvenile literature.
2. Cooks—Juvenile literature. [1. Cooks. 2. Cookery.
3. Occupations] I. Title.
TX652.J645 1985   641.5'7'023   85-11016
ISBN 0-516-01886-8

To Mom and Jeffrey

PICTURE DICTIONARY

market

bake   fry   steam   boil

recipe

spices

uniform

pastry chef

head chef

poissonier

customers

Preparing a feast in 1592 (above).
Chefs at work in 1893 (right)

4

Long ago in France, a prince planned a great feast for the king. The prince's chef cooked for twelve days and nights with no sleep. He cooked every sort of bird and beast that could be found in the land.

Finally the day of the feast arrived. But where were the fish? The chef had ordered hundreds of fish, but none had come in.

The chef knew he had failed. Without fish, the king's feast would not be complete. Quietly the chef went to his tiny room, drew his sword, and killed himself.

Today not many chefs must worry about cooking for kings. Most

chefs work in restaurants.
They cook for ordinary
people who enjoy a
good meal. Other chefs
work in hotels, schools,
hospitals—even on ships
and trains.

Chefs work hard to feed hundreds of people.

But chefs still work very hard. They may have to work from morning until late at night. They may have to work on weekends or holidays when other people are away from their jobs.

At the market a chef checks fruits and vegetables to make sure he is buying the best.

Some chefs start their workday at four or five o'clock in the morning! They go to farmers' markets and fish markets. They buy the best foods they can find to cook each day.

market

9

bake   fry   steam   boil

After chefs finish their buying, the real work begins. They look at each fruit or vegetable they bought. They look at each piece of fish or meat. Then they ask themselves questions.

"Should I bake it? Should I fry it? Should I steam it, or boil it, or just serve it raw?"

Chefs spend many hours cutting and chopping (left) before the cooking begins. Huge ovens (right) can cook dozens of dishes at once.

Chefs must know how to prepare each food so it will taste the best. They must know which spices give a certain food the best flavor.

spices

Sometimes chefs use a recipe. A recipe is a list

recipe

of directions for cooking something. But many chefs cook without recipes. They may be able to make dozens and dozens of dishes without reading directions.

Chefs must also know how to make food look good. This is called presentation. For example, they don't put

A table of food in a hotel restaurant

meat, potatoes, and vegetables on a plate just any which way. They place each food on the plate as carefully as an artist arranges colors in a painting.

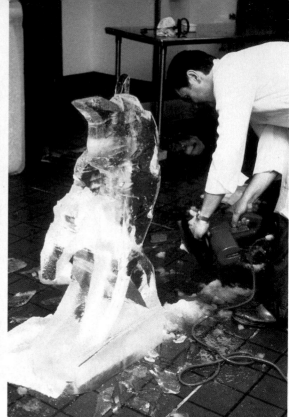

A chef in charge of soups (left) and a
chef carving ice in the shape of a bird (right)

A large restaurant may
have many chefs. Each
chef has a special job.
One chef makes soups.
One makes desserts.
One cooks fish. One
cooks meats. One

A chef with a tray of desserts (left) and a chef cutting meat (right)

makes sauces. One
makes salads. Then
there is the head chef.
The head chef is in
charge of the whole
kitchen. It is the head
chef's job to plan the

head chef

The head chef plans each day's food and gives instructions to the other chefs.

menu, or list of dishes to be served each day. The head chef also orders all the food, decides how to prepare it, and watches over the

other chefs to see that
all the food is ready
on time.

The head chef must
be able to think and act
quickly. Suppose there is
a night at the restaurant
when two hundred
people are waiting for
their dinners. The special
main dish of the day is
duck with plum sauce,
and most of the

customers

customers want that for dinner. But the sauce chef has just run out of plums.

The head chef thinks fast. "Are any fruit markets still open? Could I borrow some plums from the chef down the street? Should we just ask the people to eat something else instead?"

Some food is prepared with enormous equipment (left)
and some is prepared by hand (right).

Then the head chef
remembers that plum
tarts are on the dessert
menu that night. Would
the dessert chef please
give the sauce chef
some plums, *right now?*

The head chef has decided it is better to run out of a dessert than to run out of a main dish.

A chef who makes desserts is called a pastry chef. Pastry chefs make beautiful and tasty pies, cakes, puddings,

pastry chef

Pastry chefs make desserts that look great and taste great.

tarts, candy, cookies, and ice cream. They may get very fancy and make a dessert that looks like a flower or a swan.

One great pastry chef who lived a hundred years ago was the fanciest of all. He built giant desserts the way some people build buildings. He built desserts that looked like castles, towers, statues, fountains, and musical instruments. And everything was made out of cake, icing, sugar, and candy.

Boning fish, or taking the bones out, is a special skill.

Chefs who prepare fish are called *poissoniers* (pwah • sohn • YAYZ). (*Poisson* means "fish" in French.) They must know how to take out all the bones from a fish with

poissonier

just a few cuts of the knife. This is hard because different kinds of fish have bones in different places.

Chefs must be strong and healthy. They sometimes stand on their feet for hours. They lift heavy boxes and pots. They work where it is very hot.

Chefs wear special outfits or uniforms. They

Chefs wear white clothes and tall hats to keep cool in hot kitchens.

wear white jackets with lots of room. The white uniforms help keep the chefs cool in the kitchen. Many chefs wear a tall white hat, too. The hat works like a stovepipe. It

uniform

Students at chef schools in Austria (left) and Tahiti (right)

helps keep the chef's
head cool.

Some chefs go to chef
school to learn to cook.
Others start by working
in restaurants. They learn
on the job. As they

Julia Child, a chef who is famous all over the world, squeezing cream puffs out of a pastry bag

become better chefs, they get better jobs.

Some chefs are almost like movie stars. They write cookbooks, teach cooking classes, and have their own TV shows.

Would you like to be a
chef someday? You can
start now by using recipes
at home. Follow the
directions carefully to
cook something good
for your family and friends.

A chef shows customers a sample dish.

When they eat what you have cooked, you will know why chefs love their jobs. They love to hear people say, "Mmm, that was delicious!"

WORDS YOU SHOULD KNOW

bake (BAYK)—to cook something in the dry heat of an oven

boil (BOIL)—to cook something by putting in boiling water or other liquid

chef school (SHEF SKOOL)—a school where people learn the skills they need to be a chef

customers (KUS • tuh • murz)—people who buy something. In a restaurant, customers are buying food and the help of those who make and serve the food.

fry (FRY)—to cook in a pan that may have a little oil or fat in it. To "deep-fry" is to cook in deep oil or fat.

head chef (HED SHEF)—the chef who is in charge of a whole kitchen

menu (MEN • yoo)—a printed list of all the dishes a restaurant serves

pastry chef (PAY • stree SHEF)—a chef who makes desserts

poissonier (pwah • sohn • YAY)—a chef who prepares fish

presentation (prez • un • TAY • shun)—the way a food or several foods are arranged on a plate

raw (RAW)—not cooked

recipe (RES • uh • pee)—a list of directions for cooking something

restaurant (RES • tuh • runt)—a public eating place

sauce (SAWS)—a liquid, made of many ingredients, that adds flavor to a food

spices (SPY • siz)—plant parts or chemicals that have special flavors, used to give a food a certain taste. Salt and pepper are spices.

steam (STEEM)—to cook something in the hot vapor that rises from very hot or boiling water

uniform (YOU • nuh • form)—special clothes that people in some jobs wear

INDEX

PHOTO CREDITS

Cameramann International Ltd.—8 (right), 13, 14 (left), 15 (left), 21 (left), 26 (2 photos)

Courtesy Cunard—16

© Dan D'Attomo—9 (2 photos), 23 (left), 29

Hillstrom Stock Photo:
    © Norma Morrison—7 (right)
    © Don and Pat Valenti—23 (right), 28

Historical Pictures Service, Chicago—4 (2 photos)

Journalism Services:
    © Gregory Murphey—11 (left)

Courtesy National Restaurant Association—25 (left)

Tom Stack and Associates:
    © Sheryl S. McNee—7 (top and bottom left)

Tony Freeman Photographs/Courtesy The Anaheim Hilton—8 (left), 11 (right), 14 (right), 15 (right), 19 (2 photos), 21 (right), 25 (right)

Courtesy WGBH Educational Foundation, Boston—27

© Art Pahlke—Cover

ABOUT THE AUTHOR

Ann Heinrichs Tomchek grew up in Arkansas. She received a Bachelor of Music degree from St. Mary's College in Notre Dame, Indiana, and a Master of Music degree in Piano Performance from the American Conservatory of Music in Chicago. Ms. Tomchek has been a composer, piano recitalist, and music critic, and her reviews and feature articles have appeared in many newspapers and magazines. She is presently a freelance editor and writer, living in Naperville, Illinois, with her husband, a chef.